MILK

&

Hunny

MILK

& Hunny

Lori Gonzalez

XULON PRESS

Xulon Press
555 Winderley Pl, Suite 225
Maitland, FL 32751
407.339.4217
www.xulonpress.com

Paperback ISBN-13: 978-1-66289-982-9
Ebook ISBN-13: 978-1-66289-983-6

Dedicated to my Rudy, my devoted husband, and to our children, Anthony, Brittany, Madeline, and Cecelia. Thank you for encouraging me and making it easy for me to believe that all things are possible through Christ. You inspire me to be better every day by your examples and I'm grateful for your unending grace and kindness shown to me.

I love you bigger than the sky.

Joshua 24:15

PREFACE

On a plane ride from Camp Lejeune, North Carolina, back home to San Diego, I called my daughter and said that while I was walking through the airports, it was like walking through the halls of high school. Everywhere I looked, grandmas, my age were hurrying themselves to gates as if they were late for class. I overheard them talking to complete strangers, sharing how they too had just visited their grandchildren or were off to see them. It was very easy to pick out grandmas. Some were low-key and had expensive charm bracelets on, some were carrying grand babies alone in car seats, holding onto tiny hands, and some had monograms on their hats. But it was clear who these women were because their appearance shouted "grandma."

I told her how crowded the airports were with grandmas rushing around having panic attacks about losing their wallets, their phones, or missing their flights. She just laughed and said, "Oh, good to know, don't travel cross country in the middle of the afternoon on a Tuesday or Thursday." I said, "Yeah, unless you're a MILK or a Hunny and not in a hurry."

My first granddaughter, Bella, named me Hunny. We think it was because she heard my husband call me that but my third granddaughter, Hallie, said it was because I like sweets and I'm sweet as honey. I'll take it! My other grand-daughters Alina and Eliza make me smile just thinking of them so I will add their names here because I'm taking a grandma privilege.

My daughter said that after she gave birth to her daughter (our fifth grand-daughter), Brielle, she felt like the MILK lady. I remember those days well. It can shock your ego when you go from an independent lifestyle to suddenly having a baby as she says, "sucking the life quite literally out of you." So, we like to joke and call ourselves MILK & Hunny.

When I finally reached my gate on my second flight, I realized how empty my arms felt from not holding Brielle who was just a week shy of seven months old. I started thinking about all the grandmas I'd smiled at and seen on my brief layovers. While complete strangers, it was as if we knew each other for years. As diverse as we looked, I recognized that all of us had one mission: we must get to them.

Who? Our daughters and our granddaughters. We also shared those aching thoughts: "Did we help enough this visit?" "What do they need in between visits?" "Are they going to be okay?" Yes, we assured ourselves, they will be fine. If we could do it, surely, they could, and better.

As the wheels went up, I typed one hundred things off the top of my head that I wished I could tell my daughter between visits. When she reads this, she will probably laugh again and say, "Hunny, you have been telling me these things my whole life." I thought about all the moms out there that I have met over the years as a birth doula, pastor's wife, auntie, and mommy to three of my own. I didn't have a Hunny that taught me from the scriptures. My help has come from the LORD, mostly self-taught and self-sought.

Many mommy bloggers give good and not-so-good advice. There are also mommies, grandmas, aunties, and caregivers to encourage from the scriptures. Over the years, I have learned there are many ways to parent children. When I realized that JESUS is the ONLY way, there was so much freedom as a mommy, especially when my children were both toddlers and teenagers and I felt more like rotten MILK. I learned to discipline myself to simply pause and turn back to God so that times of refreshing would come, and they did.

As my dear friend Karen told me many years ago, "Everything you need to know on how to be a mommy is in the Bible." In this season, I'm learning how everything I need to know as a Hunny is in there, too.

Since I couldn't figure out how to extend my Wi-Fi trial session on the plane, I asked God what to do. I wrote tiny love notes with Him in mind. Then I thought, "Why not gift this to my daughter as a book? Maybe have some extras printed to share with others?" Here were the first words I typed:

> I'm going to keep writing until I get off this flight. Let's see if I get to 100 tiny love notes. Meanwhile, to all the MILKS (mommies) and all the Hunnys (grandmas, aunties, and caregivers of children), I'll be praying for you, me, yours, our grandchildren, and the children who surround us, that we will all be fine before, during, and after our visits, in JESUS name.

This book is being written in real time as I think about all the grandmas like me who can't believe all the wonders that this season of life brings and how quickly it has come. May we keep those compression socks pulled up to our knees during flights! If we get a chance to attach to the wi-fi on the plane, may we book a return trip for another visit before we land. If any of you see me in an airport, give me a shout-out. I'll be the one with the Hunny sweatshirt on. I may or may not have checked my Minnie Mouse suitcase because I'm actually making it a practice to keep clothes at my daughter's house so I have a "valid" reason to go back! My attire will scream grandma and I'll smile back at you between flights.

When the announcement came from the flight deck that it was time to power down our devices, I quickly counted how many tiny love notes I had written to MILK from Hunny… and it was exactly 100. I closed my iPad, got off the plane, and texted my daughter, "Landed."

My daughter replied, "How was your flight?"

"I wrote a book."

"I want to read it!" she replied.

"Good," I said. "It's for you."

This tiny book is meant to encourage all those who care for children.

Dear MILK,

You are LOVED.

I know that you know that, but I hope you KNOW that. For GOD so loved YOU (MILK) that HE gave His one and only Son for you (MILK) to have life.

Did you KNOW that? There's just so much good news in that. Sometimes it's hard to wrap our heads around how LOVED we are from God. Like, even more loved than we love our own little ones. But we are.

So, rest in that good news today.

~ Hunny
John 3:16

Dear MILK,

You are the apple of HIS eye.

Yup. As you look down at your precious little one, remember that God looks down on you too.

HE sees you. I'm sure HE smiles just like I do when I close my eyes and think of you.

So, smile at yourself, too.

~ Hunny
Deuteronomy 32:10

Dear MILK,

You are being held.

He's holding you in the palm of HIS hand.

However you're feeling now, remember He's got you.

HE doesn't let go.

So, breathe.

~ Hunny
John 10:29

Dear MILK,

You are not forgotten. God isn't distant nor out of reach.

HE sees you, HE hears you, HE loves you.

So, be your unforgettable self today.

~ Hunny
Ephesians 2:13

Dear MILK,

You can do it. God says that you can do ALL things through Christ who strengthens you.

HE is strengthening you at this moment. Might feel good, might not feel good just like any other workout. But you're getting stronger.

So, get after it.

~ Hunny
Isaiah 40:31

Dear MILK,

You were bought with a price.

God sent His Son to be beaten and bruised so that you don't have to beat yourself up anymore.

HE thinks you're worth it.

So, priceless one, know your worth.

~ Hunny
Isaiah 53:1-12

Dear MILK,

You are more than a conqueror.

HIS word says so.

So, warrior up.

~ Hunny
Romans 8:31-39

Dear MILK,

You can rest.

HE gives you rest. Anywhere. Anytime.

So, rest.

~ Hunny
Matthew 11:28-30

Dear MILK,

You be strong and courageous today.

No matter if it's in the big things or the little things.

HE commands it.

So, be both.

~ Hunny
Joshua 1:9

Dear MILK,

You don't let others discourage you. They aren't you.

HE is with you and commands you to not be discouraged.

So, do it.

~ Hunny
John 16:33

Dear MILK,

You are breaking generational curses every moment. How does it feel to know that?

HE cares about the generations to come.

So, keep it up!

~ Hunny
Psalm 121:1-8

Dear MILK,

You be you. God said you are fearfully and wonderfully made.

HE designed you. The Creator of the heavens and the earth designed YOU exactly how HE wanted to.

So, radiate, beaUtiful.

~ Hunny
Psalm 139:14

Dear MILK,

You are free.

JESUS broke those chains of bondage.

So, be free. Don't put them back on.

~ Hunny
Romans 8:2

Dear MILK,

You are healed.

JESUS took the stripes for your healing.

HE was wounded so you can be made whole.

So, accept it.

~ Hunny
Isaiah 53:5

Dear MILK,

You are forgiven.

JESUS cast your sins as far away as the East is from the West.

So, be forgiven and please don't forget to forgive yourself.

~ Hunny
Psalm 103:12

Dear MILK,

You are uncomfortable with the way things are? There's no need to figure anything out by yourself.

HE sent His HOLY SPIRIT to be your comforter.

So, take comfort.

~ Hunny
John 14:26

Dear MILK,

You are just getting started. No matter how young or old you are. No matter if this is the first or last baby you're caring for.

HE is molding and shaping you too.

So, don't quit, child of God.

~ Hunny
Psalm 64:8

Dear MILK,

You will go through trials.

HE says to count it all joy.

So, choose joy.

~ Hunny
James 1:2-4

Dear MILK,

You choose discretion when there's a choice to be made.

HE sees all things. Eventually, others do, too.

So, be discrete.

~ Hunny
Proverbs 2:11

Dear MILK,

You fear God. There are a lot of decisions to make.

HIS word says that the fear of God is the beginning of wisdom.

So, first, fear God before you overthink it.

~ Hunny
Proverbs 1:7

Dear MILK,

You abstain from the appearance of evil.

HE did. There's always a choice to make.

So, make good choices.

~ Hunny
1 Thessalonians 5:22

Dear MILK,

You do what's right.

HE did. Even the hard things.

So, do right before things get harder.

~ Hunny
2 Thessalonians 3:13

Dear MILK,

You rejoice. Not just during the holidays. Not just when you win.

HIS word says to rejoice in ALL things.

So, rejoice again and again.

~ Hunny
Philippians 4:4

Dear MILK,

You are to die for.

HE died so that you can live.

So, live.

~ Hunny
2 Corinthians 5:5

Dear MILK,

You go ahead and mourn. It's okay to be sad.

Jesus wept.

So, cry. Just promise you'll remember in your tears that joy is coming.

~ Hunny
John 11:35

Dear MILK,

You be found faithful. Faith comes by hearing and hearing from the word of God.

Can't find your bible? There's an app for that. I know you know where your phone is.

HIS word is life.

So, read your bible.

~ Hunny
Romans 10:17

Dear MILK,

You be obedient to the things of God.

HE demands it. Others will learn from either your obedience or your disobedience.

So, obey.

~ Hunny
John 14:15

Dear MILK,

You are made in His image.

HE doesn't make mistakes.

So, stop hating yourself.

~ Hunny
James 3:8-10

Dear MILK,

You have the armor of God.

HE tells you to put it on.

So, wear it every day and fight.

~ Hunny
Ephesians 6:10-17

Dear MILK,

You aren't your past.

HE tells you not to look back.

So, remember Lot's wife and don't look back.

~ Hunny
Luke 17:26-32

Dear MILK,

You aren't defined by your circumstances.

HE sees you through it all and calls you HIS.

So, remember who God says you are, not what the world says about you.

~ Hunny
Isaiah 43:1-7

Dear MILK,

You are enough.

HE says don't do things for the applause of others.

So, keep at it for HIS glory alone.

~ Hunny
Matthew 6:1-5

Dear MILK,

You can hear God.

HE speaks to HIS friends.

So, don't get too busy to listen.

~ Hunny
Jeremiah 33:3

Dear MILK,

You abide.

HE is carrying your burdens.

So, lighten up.

~ Hunny
John 8:31-32

Dear MILK,

You are unshakable.

HIS word says the righteous won't be shaken.

So, shake it off dear girl, just shake it off.

~ Hunny
Psalm 112:1-8

Dear MILK,

You aren't alone.

HE sees you.

So, BEloved.

~ Hunny
Genesis 16:13

Dear MILK,

You don't need to have it all figured out.

HE knows the beginning, middle, and end.

So, trust.

~ Hunny
Romans 8:28-31

Dear MILK,

You love your neighbor as yourself. Decide which one you need to work on loving more.

HE commands it.

So, as you're loving God and loving others, remember you're one, too.

~ Hunny
Mark 12:30-31

Dear MILK,

You laugh without fear of the future.

HE knows what the future holds.

So, go ahead and laugh. It's good medicine.

~ Hunny
Proverbs 31:25

Dear MILK,

You work every day. Some days or seasons, maybe for a paycheck, but every day and through every season, work for God.

HE will provide.

So, work hard.

~ Hunny
Colossians 3:23-24

Dear MILK,

You walk boldly into that throne room of grace to obtain HIS mercy.

HIS grace doesn't dry up.

So, use it.

~ Hunny
Hebrews 4:16

Dear MILK,

You receive HIS tender mercies every day. Watch the clock if you need to. At midnight rejoice that new mercies are yours!

HE sends them. It's a promise.

So, use them up.

~ Hunny
Lamentations 3:22-24

Dear MILK,

You don't grow weary for doing good.

HE tells us not to.

So, continue doing good.

~ Hunny
Galatians 6:9

Dear MILK,

You keep your home. It doesn't matter if it's small or large. Think safe. Then, think clean. Then, think cute.

HE provided your home.

So, keep it.

~ Hunny
Proverbs 24:21

Dear MILK,

You go preach the gospel.

HE commands it.

So, GO.

~ Hunny
Mark 16:15

Dear MILK,

You gather with others in sincerity.

HIS people don't need a reason to.

So, find your tribe.

~ Hunny
Acts 2:46

Dear MILK,

You have a story that can help someone else.

Whether there's happy, hard, or sad in your story, it's yours.

HE continues to write it.

So, edify others when they share theirs.

~ Hunny
Acts 9:31

Dear MILK,

You know JESUS is coming back.

HE's coming like a lion. Not a lamb.

So, be ready to hear that roar.

~ Hunny
Revelation 22:20

Dear MILK,

You have comfort. It's not from what the world gives.

HE gave you the HOLY SPIRIT.

So, be comforted.

~ Hunny
Romans 15:13

Dear MILK,

You don't have to. No matter what others may try to talk you into.

HE will give you a way out of every temptation.

So, choose HIM. Every time. Everyday. Every moment.

~ Hunny
1 Corinthians 15:33

Dear MILK,

You don't lean on someone or yourself.

HE says not even to lean on your own understanding.

So, straighten up and stand upon the ROCK.

~ Hunny
Proverbs 3:5-6

Dear MILK,

You have a voice even when you don't use it or think that you do.

HE made your mouth.

So, proclaim HIM.

~ Hunny
2 Timothy 4:2-5

Dear MILK,

You sing as if no one can hear you.

HE tells us to make a joyful noise.

So, sing!

~ Hunny
Psalm 100:1-5

Dear MILK,

You take care of the needs of others. Nothing is really ours. It's either all HIS or it's not.

HE gives generously.

So, you give cheerfully.

~ Hunny
2 Corinthians 9:6-14

Dear MILK,

You made plans? Cute.

HE orders your steps.

So, just follow HIM.

~ Hunny
Proverbs 16:9

Dear MILK,

You don't cause little ones to stumble.

HE said it would be better for you to have a millstone tied around your neck and be thrown into the ocean if you do.

So, be better.

~ Hunny
Matthew 18:6

Dear MILK,

You clothe yourself with strength and dignity.

HE calls you beautiful.

So, be dignified.

~ Hunny
Proverbs 31:25

Dear MILK,

You have been given authority to do great things.

HE said so.

So, walk in that authority.

~ Hunny
John 14:12

Dear MILK,

You be holy.

HE requires it.

So, be holy.

~ Hunny
1 Peter 1:15

Dear MILK,

You sinned? Confess.

HE already knows.

So, repent.

~ Hunny
1 John 1:9

Dear MILK,

You repented? Good.

HE longs for you to live for HIM.

So, repent and be baptized.

~ Hunny
Acts 2:38

Dear MILK,

You be zealous for the things of God.

HE is jealous for you.

So, long for Him.

~ Hunny
Galatians 4:18

Dear MILK,

You are talented.

HE gave you the ability to change someone's life.

So, don't bury your talents.

~ Hunny
Matthew 25:14-30

Dear MILK,

You never stop praying.

HE tells us to.

So, pray always, throughout the day and night.

~ Hunny
Ephesians 6:18

Dear MILK,

You have a lot to do? Those chores keep coming, I know.

HE has given you much and so much is required.

So, just do it.

~ Hunny
Luke 12:48

Dear MILK,

You are doubting?

HE said that with a mustard seed of faith, you can tell a mountain to move and it will move.

So, stop doubting and start believing.

~ Hunny
Matthew 17:20-21

Dear MILK,

You have been saved by grace.

HE said it is done.

So, don't forget what you're saved from and don't forget what you're saved to.

~ Hunny
Ephesians 2:8-10

Dear MILK,

You're tired? I know.

The best time to take a break is when you think you don't have time for one. If you don't have time for HIM then you're too busy doing stuff you don't need to.

HE gives you rest.

So, take a break.

~ Hunny
Matthew 11:28-29

Dear MILK,

You deny self more when you care for children.

HE tells us to deny self, pick up our cross, and follow Him. Don't do just one. You're already denying self.

So, now, get busy with the others.

~ Hunny
Matthew 16:24

Dear MILK,

You are adored.

HE loved you at your darkest.

So, adore HIM back.

~ Hunny
Romans 5:8

Dear MILK,

You were created for a time such as this.

HE knows everything that is going on. Nothing surprises HIM.

So, embrace it.

~ Hunny
Esther 4:14

Dear MILK,

You sought after God.

HE heard you and delivered you.

So, exalt HIS name.

~ Hunny
Psalm 34:4

Dear MILK,

You fear God, walk in HIS ways, and serve Him.

There will always be something in the way until there's not.

HE gave.

So, arise.

~ Hunny
Ezra 10:4

Dear MILK,

You do justly, love mercy, and walk humbly.

HE requires it.

So, do it.

~ Hunny
Micah 6:8

Dear MILK,

You are not forsaken.

HE is always with you.

So, be brave.

~ Hunny
 Deuteronomy 31:6

Dear MILK,

You delight in the things of the LORD.

HE will give you the desires of your heart.

So, trust in Him with all your heart, soul, mind, and strength.

~ Hunny
Psalm 37:4

Dear MILK,

You are ashamed?

HE has forgiven you.

So, shame off you.

~ Hunny
Isaiah 54:4

Dear MILK,

You are victorious.

HE doesn't give up on you.

So, endure well.

~ Hunny
Exodus 18:23

Dear MILK,

You are already loved by an unfailing love.

HE loves like no other.

So, accept it and stop looking to be loved.

~ Hunny
Jeremiah 31:3

Dear MILK,

You quench not the Spirit.

HE filled you.

So, let it loose.

~ Hunny
1 Thessalonians 5:19

Dear MILK,

You give thanks in everything.

HE is concerned about you.

So, be thankful.

~ Hunny
Philippians 4:6-7

Dear MILK,

You go prove all things.

HE asks you too.

So, start.

~ Hunny
1 Thessalonians 5:21

Dear MILK,

You hold fast to that which is good.

HE is good.

So, let the bad go and keep holding on.

~ Hunny
Hebrews 3:14

Dear MILK,

You have been called.

HE called you.

So, answer your calling.

~ Hunny
Ephesians 4:1-6

Dear MILK,

You preach the gospel fearlessly as you ought.

HE is with you.

So, don't be afraid. It's still good news.

~ Hunny
Ephesians 6:19-20

Dear MILK,

You be willing in and out of season to share your testimony.

HE will give the increase.

So, testify.

~ Hunny
2 Timothy 4:1-5

Dear MILK,

You understand and know the things of God.

HE is right.

So, walk in HIS ways.

~ Hunny
1 Kings 2:3

Dear MILK,

You are protected.

HE loves you.

So, don't be afraid.

~ Hunny
1 Corinthians 13:7

Dear MILK,

You be still. I know things are busy.

HE tells you to know that HE is GOD.

So, just be still.

~ Hunny
Psalm 46:10

Dear MILK,

You be sober-minded.

HE has great plans for you.

So, don't let anything get in the way, and don't miss out.

~ Hunny
1 Peter 5:6-11

Dear MILK,

You are powerful.

HE has given you the Holy Spirit.

So, receive it and go be a witness.

~ Hunny
Acts 1:8

Dear MILK,

You have the same Spirit inside of you that rose Christ from the grave.

HE is risen.

So, act like it.

~ Hunny
Romans 8:11-16

Dear MILK,

You have been delivered.

HE did it.

So, don't be afraid.

~ Hunny
Psalm 34:4

Dear MILK,

You have been given authority.

HE said every place your foot treads is yours to take.

So, take it.

~ Hunny
Deuteronomy 11:24

Dear MILK,

You are chosen.

HE adopted you.

So, be thankful.

~ Hunny
  Galatians 3:26-28

Dear MILK,

You have been redeemed.

HE paid the price.

So, don't count yourself short.

~ Hunny
Titus 2:11-14

Dear MILK,

You are anxious?

HE cares about you more than the birds in the air.

So, give thanks instead.

~ Hunny
Matthew 6:26-27

Dear MILK,

You're worried?

HE says not to be worried about tomorrow as today has enough of its own.

So, don't worry.

~ Hunny
Matthew 6:28-34

Dear MILK,

You keep yourself from being polluted by this world.

HE keeps you clean.

So, be clean.

~ Hunny
James 1:27

Dear MILK,

You are an image bearer.

HE is within you.

So, shine.

~ Hunny
Matthew 5:16

P.S.

MILK,

I love you. You're killin' it.

Remember where your help comes from.

BEloved,
~ Hunny

Dear Hunny,

You're killin' it too.

Don't forget these scriptures are for you, too.

I love you more.

So, you be you.

~ MILK

&

Remember God's not finished with any of you.

Philippians 1:6

Printed in the USA
CPSIA information can be obtained
at www.ICGtesting.com
CBHW081520300724
12434CB00050B/747